Introduction

How to help your pre-school child

Children learn by doing practical activities and exploring their environment. Through these experiences, they learn about the social world of people, their own bodies, movement, language and games and rules, and they will develop emotionally, physically, socially and intellectually.

This book sets out to help you to provide a variety of experiences and a stimulating environment where your child can learn through natural play situations. By doing this, you can help the child to develop basic skills in preparation for starting school.

The six areas of learning

The Foundation Stage curriculum covered by nursery and Reception classes in school is divided into six areas of learning. Nowadays, increasing numbers of other childcare settings, including playgroups, private nurseries and many registered childminders, offer similar activities that help children to work towards early learning goals in the six areas. This books contains ideas and suggestions to help your child to develop in each of the areas.

Personal, social and emotional development

Very young children are learning about people and to do so they need both to spend time alone with one adult and to share time with others. By playing and joining in with other children, they will increase their confidence. Their self-awareness will improve as they learn to be independent.

Communication, language and literacy

The activities we suggest will help children to learn to name, describe and compare things, to ask questions, give explanations and to follow instructions. Children need to be able to listen carefully and to increase their vocabulary so that they can express themselves imaginatively. Through games and practical activities, they can develop the skills necessary for learning to read and write later on.

Mathematical development

Early counting practice is very valuable, but there is more to mathematics than just number work. Numeracy activities will encourage your child's problem solving skills and logical thinking by giving them opportunities to take part in observing, collecting, sorting, comparing, matching, classifying, ordering and pattern-making.

Knowledge and understanding of the world

Young children are full of wonder and curiosity. By exploring your surroundings together you will be giving your child a valuable opportunity to develop language skills as well as motivating enthusiasm and an interest in the outside world.

Creative development

By giving children the opportunity to develop their creative skills, you are preparing them for life as well as school. The suggested activities will develop your child's observational skills and muscle co-ordination, laying a firm foundation for writing.

Physical development

Young bodies need to be active and exercised in order to develop properly and grow strong. Children need to be aware of their bodies and how to keep themselves healthy and exercise safely. We suggest a range of indoor and outdoor activities that help children to develop their balance and improve their whole-body co-ordination.

Contents

Personal, social and emotional development	2
Communication, language and literacy	4
Mathematical development	10
Knowledge and understanding of the world	14
Creative development	20
Physical development	24

Early Learning at Home | Schofield & Sims

Personal, social and emotional development

Games and play activities offer many useful opportunities for children's personal, social and emotional development. Children need to learn many social skills and become increasingly more confident and independent as they move from the home situation to childminders, playgroups, nursery and school.

Play

Children need to play:
- on their own;
- with other children;
- with adults.

Reasons for play

Play has many social and emotional benefits. It enables children to:
- become more independent;
- meet more people;
- try new challenges;
- increase their spans of attention and concentration;
- learn to control their emotions as they move towards co-operative play;
- develop socially acceptable behaviour, e.g. taking turns;
- establish friendships.

Playgroups and toddler groups

- Children often feel more secure in a small group.
- Attending a group helps them to mix and communicate with others.
- Local groups are a good introduction to nursery.

Starting school

Before starting school, children should be given opportunities to practise the social skills that will help them to gain confidence in their ability to handle different situations. You can help by ensuring that any worries are taken care of before starting school:
- Always talk positively about starting school.
- Walk past the school regularly so that your child becomes familiar with the route, the building and local area.
- If at all possible, try to meet children who will be starting school as the same time.
- Arrange visits to the class and school to meet the teachers and some of the other pupils.

Mealtimes

- These are an ideal time to get together as a family.
- They give you time to discuss the day's programme of events.
- Discourage your child from watching television whilst eating.

Parties

Invite:
- your child's friends;
- young relatives;
- neighbours' children.

Play simple games, such as:
- Pass the Parcel;
- singing games, e.g. The Farmer's in his Den;
- Musical Bumps or Statues;
- treasure hunts.

Communicating with people

Encourage your child to mix with other people. This will help your child to:
- make friends;
- play with other children;
- practise language skills.

Encourage visitors to your home:
- friends;
- relatives;
- children;
- local people.

Involve your child in your conversations with:
- the postman;
- the milkman;
- your doctor and dentist;
- their health visitor;
- community police officers.

When travelling
Take your child on train journeys, bus rides etc to extend his or her horizons. Encourage the child to:
- hand over the fare on buses, trams and trains;
- ask for the ticket.

Using the telephone
Help your child to:
- keep in touch with relatives;
- speak to friends;
- learn your telephone number.

Becoming independent

Children need to develop confidence in their own abilities and, in preparation for starting nursery and school, they need to be able to care for themselves. In particular, they need to take a growing role in looking after their bodies. Check that your child can:
- use and flush the toilet and wash hands afterwards;
- blow his or her own nose and dispose of the tissue;
- put on and take off a coat, hat, scarf and gloves;
- change shoes and socks when necessary;
- get dressed and undressed, coping with zips, buttons, laces, toggles, etc.

You could make a game of learning independence skills, for example:
- Check that your child will be able to cope with a packed lunch, unfastening a lunchbox and flask, by taking the child on two or three Teddy Bears' picnics as a 'dry run'.
- If the child has to wear shoes with laces, make a giant shoe by drawing round an adult's foot on some thick card and cutting it out. Make holes for a lace and then thread it through so your child can practise.
- Play 'Simon says' with a dressing up box, where the instructions are for putting on and taking off sweatshirts, cardigans, coats and winter 'woollies'.

Being polite
Teaching your child good manners will help him or her to get on with others.

Encourage your child to practise these skills in unpressured situations such as:
- when you go to the park or beach;
- at the swimming baths or soft play;
- when staying with a friend or visiting relatives

Communication, language and literacy

Through play and a variety of activities, children will learn:
- to name, describe and compare things, to ask questions and give explanations;
- to follow instructions;
- an increased vocabulary;
- imagination and self-expression;
- about the structure of sentences;
- how to use verbs, nouns, adjectives, adverbs and prepositions;
- skills that are needed for reading and writing, and the necessary hand and eye co-ordination.

Speaking and listening

Talking is an important part of learning! Listening is part of talking. Children need to be stimulated and encouraged to talk and to listen:
- Talk with your child about everyday routines such as bath time and mealtimes, and things around them like tools, equipment and kitchen utensils and their uses.
- Encourage them to explain situations and why they happen, e.g. a burst pipe.
- Use the correct words – children enjoy the sounds of new terms and are very quick to pick up long words.
- Correct grammatical mistakes in a pleasant, non-threatening way, repeating sentences correctly.
- Ask children to recall incidents, a story or a television programme, and to guess what might happen next.
- Puppets are simple to make, and even shy children will often speak through another character.

At home
Talk to your child as you work and play together, for example when:
- cleaning the car;
- baking;
- gardening;
- doing creative activities;
- hanging out the washing;
- talking to friends and relatives on the phone.

Away from home
Visits to parks and other places of interest not only encourage curiosity about the world, but also increase children's powers of observation, their vocabulary and memory. Ask questions like:
- "What happened when we went to the theme park?"
- "How did we get there?"
- "Which ride did you like best?"
- "What was it like on the water splash?"

Developing a wider vocabulary
Children may find some new concepts difficult to understand, so whenever possible use words in practical situations. This will help your child's vocabulary. Repeated use in conversation will help with their understanding.

For example, you can help your child to learn positional words and opposites with the following:
- "Bounce the big ball."
- "Throw me the little ball."
- "Look, the cat is in the basket."
- "Take your boat out of the bath."
- "Put teddy between two cars."
- "Jump through the hoop."
- "Climb up the steps, then come down the slide."
- "Run round the garden."
- "Crawl under the table."
- "Put a hat on teddy."
- "Take your scarf off."
- "It's raining outside, but we are inside."
- "Walk 10 steps backwards, then skip five steps forwards."
- "Open the cupboard."
- "Shut the door."

Following instructions

This will help your child to listen carefully and to remember things: for example, messages. Give one instruction at first, then slowly increase the difficulty of the message:
- "Tell Daddy his tea is ready."
- "Tell Mummy she's wanted on the phone."
- "Give the dog his dinner, then take him for a walk."
- "Please go upstairs and find your book and give it to your sister."

This can be developed by asking your child to play fun games, which will also be good for co-ordination:
- "Put your hand on your head and pat it."
- "Rub your tummy and jump up and down."
- "Put your hands on your knees and walk backwards."
- "Lie on your back, put your legs in the air and pretend to cycle".

Remembering things

Encouraging your child to remember simple things can be a good foundation for remembering sounds, words and spellings later on. Games can be a good way of developing children's imagination, memory and eventually their story-writing skills.

Talking games

These can be great fun! A good starter is "I saw an elephant in the garden!" The child then has to add another sentence. You can give encouragement by prompting with such questions as:
- "What did he do?"
- "How big was he?"
- "Who was with him?"

Chinese Whispers

Play this game with a few children. The first has to whisper a word or short phrase to the person next in the circle. The last person shouts out the word. Older children can be asked to pass on longer sentences.

Kim's Game

Put a few objects or toys on a tray. Ask your child to look at them and talk about them together. Next, ask your child to leave the room or look away while you remove one thing from the tray. Does your child know which one is missing? Make the game harder by adding more objects, by removing two of them, or by moving them round on the tray.

Can you remember?

Choose four picture cards and put them out in a row. Encourage your child to look at them carefully and talk about them. Ask the child to hide their eyes while you remove a card. Ask them to describe which card is missing. Another time, alter the order of the cards, then ask the child to put them back in the correct order. You could also try this game with toys.

The shopping game

Take it in turns to say "I went to the shops and bought a_____." Each person playing has to remember each item 'bought' in the right order before adding another item, until someone forgets!

Extend the fun by making a longer rhyme for children to remember:
"Going to the shops,
Going to the shops,
I saw (a dinosaur)
Going to the shops!"

Encourage your child to think of different people, animals or situations to remember. After a while, the above rhyming game could be extended by adding an adjective, e.g. to "a green dinosaur".

Communication, language and literacy

Reading

It is a good idea to set aside a few minutes each day to read with your child. Increase the length of the session as children grow older. Enjoyable activities can give your child a good start with learning to read and can help them to develop a love of books:

- When reading books together, point to the words as you read.
- Read favourite stories many times so that your child will memorise the story; this is a key stage in learning to read.
- Pause before certain words and let your child fill them in.
- Bedtime stories are important – not only do they help the child to sleep, but they are also a good introduction to the pleasure of reading books.
- Play 'Snap' using pictures of rhyming words, encouraging your child to say each word on putting down the card.
- Involve your child in helping you to look up information from an early age; for example, to use dictionaries and reference books.
- Before starting school, it is useful if all children can recognise their own names.

Read a range of books together

Children enjoy reading storybooks and picture books and many like to interact with pop-up books and those that include sound effects and moving parts. Poems and nursery rhymes, fairy tales and traditional stories are fun but also widen children's experience. Non-fiction is also important, and there are books to help children learn about colours, numbers, shapes, sizes and the alphabet.

As well as books, you can read a variety of everyday things, including:
- adverts;
- food packets;
- comics;
- road signs;
- shop names;
- birthday cards.

Looking at pictures

Looking at pictures together helps to establish children's powers of observation. Talk about the pictures and ask relevant questions:
- "Can you see the bird?"
- "Where is it?"
- "What is it doing?"
- "What colour is it?"
- "Who is watching?"
- "What do you think could happen next?"

Make a picture book

Cut out pictures from magazines, postcards and birthday cards and stick them in a scrapbook. You could include photographs of family members, friends and your child's visits to interesting places. Write the child's own words underneath the pictures. Keep the book accessible so that your child can look at it alone or choose things to add to the book.

The star of story time

Story time is a special time for parents and children to share. Take the opportunity for story telling whenever possible. Children love stories about themselves. For example, you can start a story using your child as the main character:

"Once upon a time, there was a little child called _____."

Your child will enjoy adding to the story, and you can make it great fun!

Getting interested in books

Show that you have an interest in books by letting your child see you read. This will have a lasting influence on the child's reading.

Visit bookshops and the local library together. 'Children's corners' are attractive and there may be special storytelling events to attend.

Look at and talk about the books, allowing your child to choose a picture or story book to buy or borrow.

Choose a book for yourself to encourage your child to borrow books from the library.

If your child has a particular interest, e.g. in tractors, find some information books about the subject.

Some useful pre-reading activities

Activities such as these can help your child to prepare for learning to read. You can devise them yourself, using household objects and toys, pencil and paper. You could also buy puzzle books with similar activities in them.

Spot the difference:
- "Which is the odd one out?"
- "Which is different?"
- "Point to the two that are the same."

Left to right
These pencil and paper exercises help to familiarise the child's hand and eye to move the correct way across the page:
- "Show me which way the car goes to the garage."
- "Which way is the cat going to her dish?"

Observational skills:
- "Make these the same."
- "Use string to join the ones that match."
- "What can you see in the tangled picture?"
- "Use your finger to show the way through the maze."

Sequences and patterns:
- "Make a pattern the same as mine."
- "Now make the pattern longer by adding the right objects."

Rhyme time
Rhyme is one of the most important pre-reading elements. Young children who hear rhymes generally learn to read more quickly. Encourage your child to listen for rhymes in words and sentences. It is a good idea to introduce this by using familiar objects. For example:

chair   bear

pear   hair

Recite or sing lots of nursery rhymes and read rhyming books, e.g. *The Cat in the Hat* by Dr Seuss.

Find a rhyme for your child's name, such as 'Alice from the palace', or make up a fun nonsense rhyme, e.g. 'Garry-Arry'. The story of Henny Penny will give you plenty of ideas!

It's good fun making up your own rhyming sentences:
- "Fred's in bed with a sore head."
- "He saw a bee in a tree by the sea when he was eating his tea!"

Communication, language and literacy

Letter sounds

Phonics play a vital part in learning to read and spell. Listen out for sounds in words. Play 'I spy!' together. Sounds in words are called phonemes. Some sounds are made of single letters and others have more than one letter, e.g. 'tr' and 'ee' in 'tree'.

Often, letter names are different from the sound the letter makes when it is pronounced. When playing sound games, use the sounds the letter makes:

- a as in apple;
- b as in ball;
- c as in cup;
- d as in dog;
- e as in egg;
- f as in fish;
- g as in gate;
- h as in house;
- i as in igloo;
- j as in jelly;
- k as in kite;
- l as in lemon;
- m as in mouse;
- n as in net;
- o as in orange;
- p as in pan;
- q as in queen;
- r as in rainbow;
- s as in sun;
- t as in tortoise;
- u as in umbrella;
- v as in vase;
- w as in windmill;
- x as in fox;
- y as in yacht;
- z as in zebra.

Writing

Clear handwriting develops from good manual control, which can be encouraged in many ways. The following activities can help:

- playing with playdough or Plasticine®;
- finger painting;
- cutting and sticking;
- doing jigsaws;
- playing with bricks and other constructional toys;
- throwing and catching balls;
- tracing;
- drawing round templates and shapes;
- colouring;
- painting;
- making patterns.

Early beginnings

Help your child to understand the uses for writing by sharing:

- lists;
- cards;
- letters;
- invitations;
- stories;
- books;
- poems;
- diaries;
- instructions;
- recipes;
- messages;
- labels.

Encourage your child's pre-writing skills by setting up the following activities:

- Play with wooden and plastic letters, including magnetic ones on your fridge.
- Trace your fingers over sandpaper letters.
- Sprinkle some salt or fine sand on a tray to just cover the surface, and then practise patterns with your finger.
- Make marks on paper with a thick pencil or felt tip pen.

- Scribble different coloured patterns on paper.
- Take a pencil 'for a walk' across a page.
- Encourage your child's eyes to move from left to right across the page.
- Make patterns that will be needed later for letter formation.
- Draw round your hand, keeping the first three fingers together. Add a beak and an eye, then cut out your bird and hang it up with cotton.

Making writing easier
- Provide a range of media to practise writing, including paper of different sizes, colours and textures, notebooks, a range of chunky pencils, crayons, pens and felt tips with safety caps, chalk and chalkboard, and a whiteboard with marker pens.
- A pencil grip is a good buy as it can help a child to hold a pencil correctly.

- It is often difficult for a young child to hold anything still whilst drawing round it or to keep the paper steady when writing, so use a little bit of sticky tape or Blu-Tack® to hold things in position.
- If your child is left-handed, don't try to change this. Encourage the child to place the paper at an angle that makes it easier to write.
- If you teach your pre-school child to write his or her own first name, only use a capital letter at the beginning and write in lower case for the rest of the name. Don't use capitals throughout.
- Only use capital letters for names, proper nouns and at the beginnings of sentences.
- Check which handwriting style is used in your child's school when teaching the letters of the alphabet, and start with lower-case letters first.

Mathematical development

Games and play activities offer many useful opportunities for the development of children's maths skills, including:
- counting;
- understanding one-to-one correspondence;
- arranging things in order;
- sorting by colour, shape and size;
- classifying;
- basic measurement;
- simple time concepts;
- making patterns.

Counting

Help your child to be aware of numbers in everyday life. Start with counting to five, then ten and so on.

Things to count with your child

Take every possible chance to count:
- buttons on clothes;
- steps and stairs;
- windows, doors, lights, chairs, etc;
- people in a queue or waiting room;
- tins, groceries and pieces of fruit;
- toys, including vehicles, balls, soft toys and building bricks;
- cups, saucers, mugs, plates and cutlery;
- books, magazines and comics;
- candles on a birthday cake;
- ducks on a pond;
- objects in pictures and books;
- the chimes of a clock.

Other things to help your child's awareness of numbers

Look out for any opportunities to draw your child's attention to:
- house numbers and postcodes;
- telephone numbers;
- ages on a birthday card;
- a calendar;
- the numbers on a clock;
- page numbers when sharing a book;
- dice and number games;
- weights on packets and tins;
- numbers on scales;
- rulers and tape measures;
- numbers on your computer;
- prices displayed in shops and adverts;
- bus numbers;
- car registration numbers;
- distances on signposts.

Counting games, rhymes and stories

Many children's games have a counting theme, or you could invent some of your own:
- Snakes and Ladders;
- Ludo;
- Junior Monopoly;
- How many steps?
- How many balls can you throw into a basket or container?

Finger rhymes and nursery rhymes with a counting theme are always enjoyable. They give lots of valuable repetition, and the use of fingers to assist the rhyme helps with one-to-one correspondence.

Examples include:
- One, two three, four, five, Once I caught a fish alive;
- Five little ducks went swimming one day;
- Peter plays with one hammer;
- Two little dicky birds sitting on a wall;
- Ten fat sausages frying in a pan;
- This old man, he played one;
- Ten green bottles.

Stories with numbers in them help children to see how numbers are used in familiar contexts. Look out for versions of:
- The Three Little Pigs;
- Goldilocks and the Three Bears;
- The Billy Goats Gruff;
- Snow White and the Seven Dwarfs.

Games using money

Help your child to become familiar with how money is used by:
- counting 1p coins;
- matching different coins of different values;
- sorting a pile of real coins or realistic play money;
- playing shops using amounts up to 10p in 1p coins.

Sorting, matching and classifying

Help your child to sort objects into groups by:
- colour;
- size;
- shape.

Things your child could sort:
- household objects, such as buttons;
- groceries – putting all the tins of beans together, then all the bottles of juice;
- fruit and vegetables;
- cutlery;
- toys like vehicles, soft toys, farm animals and construction bricks and shapes;
- leaves and flowers;
- clean laundry – finding all the T-shirts or pairing socks;
- books;
- coins.

Sorting and matching games

Often children don't notice that they are doing maths when they play games such as:
- Dominoes;
- Pairs;
- Happy Families or Fours;
- Snap – with pictures, shapes or numbers;
- many games using dice.

You can invent your own activities to develop your child's sorting and matching skills.

Ask the child to match the things that belong together. Use everyday things from around the house:
- differently shaped objects;
- toys;
- shoes;
- pictures;
- bricks;
- balls.

Using pencil and paper, draw three dogs and three bones. Ask the child to give each dog a bone by drawing a line from one to the other. Think of other ideas, such as cups and saucers or eggs and eggcups.

Early Learning at Home | Schofield & Sims

Mathematical development 11

Mathematical development

Learning colours

It is helpful if your child knows at least some colours before starting school. Start by talking about the things around you:
- "Let's put on your red T-shirt today."
- "Can you see the big yellow sun in the sky?"
- "Here is a juicy green apple to eat."
- "What colour is our car?"
- "Point to the white fence in this picture."

Talking about size

Again, you can talk together as you share activities:
- "The dessert spoons are big but the teaspoons are small."
- "The pencil is longer than the crayon."
- "Who is the tallest in our family?"
- "Which is wider – the road or the footpath?"

Looking at shapes

First make sure that your child can recognise simple two-dimensional shapes:
- square;
- circle;
- triangle;
- rectangle.

Look at shapes around the house and use them to do fun activities:
- Draw round shaped bricks to make pictures of objects such as a house, a tree or a car.
- Print pictures by painting different shapes or do vegetable printing with potatoes or carrots.

Measuring

Before children learn to use traditional measurements, they benefit from experiencing other ways of measuring:
- measuring height, width or length using handspans or footsteps;
- weighing using building bricks or pine cones;
- measuring capacity with different sizes and shapes of containers, plastic bottles or eggcups;
- gauging time by counting, e.g. when playing Hide and Seek.

Talk about measuring to develop your child's mathematical vocabulary:
- "How tall are you?"
- "How long is this skipping rope?"
- "Is this bookshelf wider than your desk?"

Encourage your child to use a balance to weigh different quantities of items such as:
- dried peas and pasta;
- seashells and pebbles;
- pencils or crayons;
- building bricks or toys;
- grocery packets;
- letters and parcels.

Ask:
- "Which is heavier?"
- "Which is lighter?"
- "Can you guess which will weigh more?"

Set up water play in a washing-up bowl, sink, bath or paddling pool, and ask:
- "Is this jug full or empty?"
- "How many cups of water would it take to fill the bottle half way?"
- "Would all of the water in this bottle fit into your jam jar?"

Time

Again, your child will learn a basic concept of time through talking about activities as they are happening, recalling events that have already taken place, and looking forward to things that will be done in the future. Discuss:
- Days of the week – which days do you go to playgroup, nursery or school and which do you stay at home?
- Times of the day – what time does the child go to bed or when is our favourite television programme on?
- Months – talk about birthdays and look forward to important festivals.
- The seasons – when do the leaves fall off the trees, when is the weather coldest, when do we go on holiday, etc?

Talk about:
- the difference between analogue and digital clocks;
- how long an activity or journey might take;
- what time it is – ask your child to guess.

Use 'time' words and terms in conversations with your child, for example:
- today;
- yesterday;
- tomorrow;
- now;
- soon;
- later;
- last week;
- next week.

Patterns and sequences

Being asked to identify patterns and sequences helps your child to develop and use mental maths skills. It also promotes thinking skills such as logic that will be useful in other areas of learning, including literacy skills needed for reading, writing and giving instructions and explanations.

Some objects to use for patterns and sequences include:
- interlocking cubes;
- building blocks of different colours;
- threading beads;
- shapes;
- leaves;
- cutlery;
- toy cars;
- soft toys;
- groceries;
- picture cards;
- books.

Sequencing activities:
- Ask your child to copy a pattern that you have made.
- Ask what should come next.
- Muddle up the pattern and ask the child to make the same pattern that you made originally.
- Can the child think up a new pattern?
- Look for patterns around the house, for example in fabrics and wallpapers.
- Keep an eye out for patterns in the street or when you visit friends and family, for example brickwork, paving stones, tiling and patios.

Knowledge and understanding of the world

Children are naturally curious about the world around them. They like exploring their home environment, and can learn about how things work from even the simplest journey such as a walk to the local shop or park. Your area will have many places to visit. You can also set up many enjoyable games and activities at home.

The five senses

Stimulating children's senses helps to prepare them for learning. It encourages curiosity and an understanding of the environment.

Hearing

Children enjoy sounds. Encourage your child to listen. Is it possible to recognise sounds without seeing the source?

Enjoy:
- holding a shell to your ear to find out what you can hear;
- distinguishing between water sounds, such as a tap dripping, a bath emptying, pebbles being dropped into water, a fountain or sprinkler, rain falling and waves at the seaside;
- closing your eyes and guessing sounds like a doorbell ringing, the telephone, a toilet flushing, keys jangling, a door banging, footsteps, or money in a pocket.

Listen to garden sounds:
- birds singing;
- bees buzzing;
- leaves rustling;
- a hedge-trimmer droning;
- a lawnmower whirring.

Listen to kitchen sounds:
- a kettle boiling;
- a microwave 'pinging';
- the washing machine;
- the tumble dryer;
- a food mixer.

Different uses of voices:
- talking;
- laughing;
- whispering;
- singing;
- shouting;
- speaking through a cardboard tube;
- talking through a paper or toy megaphone.

Recognising animal sounds:
- a dog barking;
- a cat meowing;
- a pigeon cooing;
- a duck quacking;
- a bird singing;
- a cow mooing.

Record some different noises for your child to guess:
- a car engine starting;
- a motorbike;
- a police siren;
- an ice-cream van;
- a vacuum cleaner;
- someone clapping;
- a baby crying.

Seeing

Draw your child's attention to everyday things. Describe things and encourage your child to do the same. Ask questions such as:
- "Can you see that red tractor?"
- "What is it doing?"
- "What else can you see?"

REMEMBER: Never, ever, look directly at the sun!

Things to do:
- Look through binoculars and describe what you can see.
- Look through a magnifying glass or microscope to enlarge a slice of lemon or a piece of pepper.
- Look through a kaleidoscope and watch the patterns change.
- Play hide and seek – can you see where the others are hiding?
- Play Snap and other matching games.
- Make patterns when playing with building blocks – can your child copy them?
- Play 'I spy' with colours or shapes instead of sounds.

Look at reflections in:
- mirrors;
- windows;
- shiny surfaces;
- cooking foil;
- puddles;
- both sides of spoons;
- any shiny tin.

Smelling

This is often the most difficult sense for children to appreciate. Try wearing a blindfold for these activities – then your sense of smell will be heightened.

Things to do:
- Ask your child to distinguish between different smells – just two at first, increasing as confidence develops.

Set up a 'smelling table' with a range of smells:
- perfume or soap;
- mint or toothpaste;
- polish;
- strawberries;
- apple;
- garlic or onion;
- fish;
- cheese;
- flowers;
- lemons;
- lavender;
- scented candles or pot-pourri.

Tasting

Our taste buds help us to distinguish between different tastes – sweet, sour, bitter etc. Again, wear a blindfold before trying different things. Set up a 'taste table', using clean yoghurt pots or saucers to keep the flavours separate. Try all of these and more:
- cheese;
- lemon juice;
- orange juice;
- apple or pear;
- fish;
- different coloured sweets;
- chocolate;
- crisps;
- onion.

Touching

'DO NOT TOUCH' is a common warning, but children need to be involved in tactile play. From babyhood, they naturally feel and touch things to explore them. This is one of the first ways they learn. Even adults like to touch new things or feel something furry or shiny!

Things to do:
- Feel soft things such as cotton wool, feathers and fabrics.
- Touch hard things like pottery, crystal, nails, bricks and metal.
- Carefully feel rough things, including the bristles on a brush, a pan scrubber or soap pad, a grater and the bark of a tree.
- Stroke furry things such as fur fabric and real or toy animals like a dog, cat or rabbit.
- Feel smooth things like silk, glass, foil, silverware, or an eggshell.
- Set up a table with some of these things for your child to touch.
- Go for a 'touching walk' – feel twigs, leaves, flowers, tree bark, stones, pebbles and bricks.
- Play 'Simon says' and touch your toes, knees, shoulders, etc.
- Make a 'feely bag' from a remnant of fabric or use a shoe-bag or empty cushion cover – fill with small objects and see if your child can guess what they are just by feeling them (without looking!).

Knowledge and understanding of the world

Exploring

Your child will enjoy exploring different environments, and will learn without realising!

Parks and gardens:
- Observe changes according to the weather, months and seasons.
- Talk about and collect leaves, conkers, acorns, cones, seed heads, twigs, and pieces of bark that have fallen to the ground.
- Make daisy chains, pressed flower pictures, a wormery, and collections, for example of rough and smooth things.
- What can you see in a park – a play area, tennis courts or bowling green, a pond?
- Discuss which tools you use for different gardening jobs, and what you wear in the garden.
- Encourage your child to help with planting seeds or bulbs, to dig and rake, and to feel the textures of potting compost, stones, tree trunks, leaves and plants.
- Count how many birds, insects, minibeasts, trees or flowers you can recognise.

Roads:
- Count houses, lamp posts and gates and look at door numbers.
- Look at and discuss roadworks, traffic lights and pedestrian crossings.
- Talk about road signs, junctions and roundabouts.
- Which buses go near your street, and where are they going?
- Spot different kinds of vehicles, including the emergency services.
- Look for traffic wardens and police officers – what jobs do they do?
- Emphasise road safety. Observe the Green Cross Code, and make sure your child can cross a road safely.

Towns:
- Take a journey by bus, tram, metro, underground or railway – let your child help to buy the tickets.
- When shopping, ask your child to help you to look out for shops and supermarkets, your bank or post office, the car park or a parking meter.

Find out what different shops sell:
- supermarket;
- newsagent;
- jeweller;
- florist;
- bakery;
- delicatessen;
- butcher;
- fishmonger;
- stationer;
- chemist;
- DIY store;
- sports shop;
- the local 'take away'.

Look at buildings and talk about their use:
- factories;
- warehouses;
- shops and supermarkets;
- shopping malls;
- cinemas and theatres;
- museums and art galleries;
- libraries;
- playgroups, nurseries and schools;
- medical centres and hospitals;
- the leisure centre and swimming pool;
- places of worship of different religions;
- restaurants and cafés;
- the fire station and police station.

Animals

Most children love animals. Encourage your child to respect animals and treat them well.

ALWAYS make sure children wash their hands after handling animals.

Pets:
- If you are able to have a pet in your family, give your child a chance to help to care for it.
- Your child will enjoy helping you to feed, groom and exercise an animal, and will learn about taking responsibility.
- Pets can give children valuable experience of birth, life and death.

Birds:
- In winter, you could feed birds in your garden to encourage them to use a bird table – your child could help with this.
- Watch birds and try to identify them using a simple bird book.
- Put up a nesting box, but remind your child not to touch the nest or take the eggs – talk about why!
- Put out water for the birds and watch them drink and bathe.
- Count the number of birds you see.
- Visit the ducks in your local park, pond or river.

Minibeasts:
- Look under stones or logs in your garden and talk about what you can see.
- Find a spider's web and discuss why spiders spin webs.
- Count the number of legs on a spider, beetle or butterfly.
- Look at ladybirds and count their spots – are they all the same?
- Watch worms wriggling, caterpillars nibbling and snails leaving a trail.
- Look at butterflies and moths, and talk about their symmetrical wings.
- Look at the spiral pattern on a snail's shell.
- Watch bees gathering pollen.

Farm animals:
- Visit a city farm or pets' corner, or take a trip into the countryside if you are not near to a farm.
- Some of these places have open days where children can observe and handle smaller animals.
- Talk about what the animals eat and what they give us.
- Make a book about farm animals – stick in pictures and write in words connected with them.

Zoo animals:
- Views on whether animals should be kept in zoos vary – talk to your child about this.
- A well managed zoo or safari park with modern enclosures and conservation programmes can give your child a chance to see a wide range of animals.
- Discuss what the animals eat and what their natural habitat is.
- Find out what your child's favourite animal is and why.
- Make a Wild Animal Book or poster, using pictures or drawings, or make a plan of the zoo you visited.

Plants

You can look at plants in your garden or local park, at a garden centre or in a wood or forest area.

Trees:
- Look at trees at different times of year – how do they change?
- Talk about which are the tallest and smallest.
- Use a tree book from the library to help you identify the trees.
- Collect leaves to press or to use for leaf rubbings, then use to make a leaf picture.
- Press some paper against the trunk of a tree and rub wax crayon over it to make a bark rubbing – compare rubbings from different trees.

Knowledge and understanding of the world

Plants and bulbs:
- Try growing cress in different places, for example in an empty eggshell.
- Grow your own peas and beans – soak dried ones well before planting.
- Plant seeds and bulbs and watch them grow.
- Let your child help you to water houseplants or the garden.

Fruit and vegetables:
- Make vegetable prints – cut the vegetable in half, saturate a sponge with paint and press the vegetable onto the sponge. Then print onto paper.
- Talk about how fruit and vegetables grow – buy a stick of sprouts, some tomatoes on the vine or a bunch of bananas and look at their growth pattern.
- Cut an onion, pepper, apple or kiwi fruit in half and look at the patterns.
- Collect seeds (such as from an apple) or tops (like carrot or pineapple tops) and plant them on a saucer to see how they grow.
- Name fruits and vegetables when you are at the greengrocer or supermarket.
- Taste some of the more unusual fruit and vegetables and talk about them.

Hot and cold

Children enjoy learning by doing simple experiments and investigations. They will start to learn about science if you help them to do the following activities:
- Discuss what happens to ice cubes – put some in a bowl in a warm place and some in the fridge. Compare what happens to each.
- Take a walk on a frosty day to look at the trees – what happens to your breath when you breathe out? Does the same thing happen indoors?
- Discuss temperatures – take your child's temperature. Why does the doctor sometimes take your temperature?
- Look at a thermometer – touch the bottom and see what happens.
- What clothes do we wear in winter – are they the same as summer clothes?

Water

All children are fascinated by water and enjoy water play. They do need to know safety rules when near water.

NEVER leave your child unsupervised, even near the shallowest water.

Floating and sinking:
- Half fill a washing-up bowl or baby's bath with water and encourage your child to experiment with water toys such as boats and ducks.
- Find out which of these things sink and which float – balls, corks, stones, rubber bands, wooden bricks, plastic toys, coins, keys, a sieve.

Bubbles:
- Blow bubbles and watch how far they float before bursting.
- What happens when they burst?
- Where might you see bubbles?
- Put bubbles in your child's bath.
- Ask your child to put a straw in soapy water and blow down it – what happens? (But supervise to make sure the child doesn't suck instead!)

Puddles:
- Put on wellingtons and splash in a puddle.
- Look at different puddles.
- What makes a puddle?
- What happens to a puddle when the sun shines?

Weather

Weather affects everyone! Discuss the weather throughout the year with your child, deciding together the most suitable clothes to wear each day.

Things to do:
- Hang a fir cone outside your door or window, and talk about what happens to the cone on different days.
- Make a simple weather chart for a week, then count the number of sunny or wet days.
- Watch the weather forecast together – talk about the symbols used. Was the forecast accurate?
- Talk about the changes in weather you can expect in each new month – relate this to birthdays, festivals, sporting events, things happening in the garden, etc.
- Day and night – is it colder at night or at mid-day? Talk about when it is dark – does the weather affect this?

The seasons

Talk about the four seasons. Take the same walk each season so that you can observe the changes. 'Adopt' a particular tree so that you can note the differences.

In spring, look out for:
- warmer days;
- buds;
- seeds growing;
- bulbs;
- blossom;
- birds nesting;
- new baby lambs.

In summer, look out for:
- trees in leaf;
- flowers blooming;
- sunny weather;
- holiday-makers;
- longer, lighter days;
- people watering gardens.

In autumn, look out for:
- nuts and berries;
- colour of foliage;
- leaves falling;
- harvest;
- birds migrating;
- days getting cooler;
- bonfires.

In winter, look out for:
- cold weather;
- snow;
- frost;
- ice;
- fog;
- bare trees;
- shorter days.

Colour

The world would be very different without any colour!

Things to do:
- Collect toys and objects of the same colour and display on a table covered in fabric of the same colour – change the colour each week until your child knows them all.
- Make a Colour Book – for example, cut out pictures of things that are red and stick them in.
- Play colour games – for example, "I spy with my little eye something that is green".
- Sort buttons or bricks into groups of the same colour, then make it harder by sorting each group into light and dark shades.
- Discuss which colour is your child's favourite and why.
- Which colour does your child wear most often? You could keep a chart for a week to find out.
- Look out for a rainbow when it has rained – talk about the colours and what order they come in (red, orange, yellow, green, blue, indigo, violet).
- Make a rainbow spinner using a 10cm circle of card. Divide the circle into seven equal sections. Use felt tips or crayons to colour each section with a colour of the rainbow. Put a pencil through the centre and spin to see what happens.
- Talk sensitively to your child about colour and ourselves – people have many things the same, but some things are different colours, including hair, eyes and skin.

Early Learning at Home | Schofield & Sims

Knowledge and understanding of the world 19

Creative development

Children enjoy learning from artistic and often very messy activities! Through taking part in these activities, and by using different materials, they will develop:
- their creativity;
- hand-eye co-ordination;
- their hand and arm muscles;
- their powers of observation;
- concentration;
- imagination;
- the ability to explore shape, space, size and colour;
- a feeling for texture;
- concepts of number and language;
- the ability to share with others and take turns.

Many different types of play help to develop a child's creativity, for example:
- picture making and printing;
- cutting and sticking;
- model making, including three-dimensional projects;
- craft activities, such as sewing;
- movement and dance to different types of music and sounds;
- making up songs and poems;
- rhythm and music making;
- make-believe and dramatic play.

Developing independence
Young children may need to be shown how to do things at first, but they should be encouraged to do things for themselves whenever possible.

They will be proud of their projects if they have done them independently. The more practical experience children have, the better they become and the quicker they will learn.

By all means help your child, but then try to stand back and observe. Words of encouragement and questions such as "How do you think it should be stuck together?" are much better than performing the task yourself.

Ask your child to explain their artwork to you – this is good experience for them but also avoids you guessing wrongly!

Ensuring safety
When preparing to do creative activities with your child, think about a few safety issues:
- Consider providing protective clothing such as an apron, overall or an old shirt, or wear old clothes that you don't mind getting messy.
- When painting or gluing, cover the table or work surface with newspaper or a plastic tablecloth.
- Always use child-friendly non-toxic glues – preferably washable.
- Ensure that all pens and felt-tips have ventilated safety caps.
- Devise some basic rules that are easy to remember, for example when working with scissors the child is not allowed to walk around carrying them, and knives must be passed blade down.

Painting and printing

Start off by:
- using one colour only at first;
- increasing the number of colours gradually;
- providing a separate brush for each pot;
- washing dirty brushes regularly;
- encouraging your child to experiment with mixing colours by putting a blob of each colour on a white paper plate.

Paint on:
- newspaper;
- the back of wallpaper;
- lining paper;
- a plastic surface such as a tray.

Print with:
- fingers, hands and feet;
- sponges cut into different shapes;
- pastry cutters;
- polystyrene packaging;
- wooden blocks;
- corks, keys and buttons;
- cotton reels and yoghurt pots;
- cut vegetables such as potatoes and carrots.

Painting techniques:
- Make paint thicker by adding a little fine sand or flour to the paint.
- Cover a surface with paint using a sponge, then ask your child to use their fingers to make marks or to draw with their fingers.
- Draw a picture or make a pattern with wax crayons then cover with a weak wash of paint and see what happens.

Printing activities:
- Apply paint onto the child's hands or feet with a sponge, then print with them.
- Pour paint onto a sponge in a margarine tub, press your chosen objects onto the sponge and then print.
- Pre-prepare different sponge shapes, then clip a peg to each for your child to use as a 'handle'.

Cutting, sticking and collage

Using scissors:
- Buy a good pair of scissors – cheap ones may not cut as well.
- Good toyshops sell scissors for both left- and right-handed children.
- You might need to hold the paper at first.
- Encourage your child to practise on old magazines and birthday cards.
- Things the child has cut out can then be stuck onto paper and made into a book.

Sticking:
- Always choose a child-friendly non-toxic glue that is washable for spills on clothing.
- Glue sticks are good for sticking two bits of lighter paper together.
- Liquid glue is better for heavier paper and thin card.
- PVA glue is best for heavier card.
- Sticky tape can be doubled over to make it double-sided.
- Parcel tape is excellent for sticking cardboard from cereal boxes or packaging.

Materials for collage:
- pasta and pulses;
- sequins, buttons and pipecleaners;
- string and wool;
- screw-on bottle tops and corks;
- tissue paper and gift-wrap;
- cellophane and foil;
- leaves and acorns;
- flowers and grasses;
- shells and cleaned feathers;
- all kinds of fabric;
- packaging 'squiggles' and bubble wrap.

Ideas for cutting, sticking and collage projects:
- Make a paper mat by folding a square or rectangle of paper into quarters. Cut out shapes along the folded edge. Open up to see the pattern. Use a circle of paper if you want to make a doily or snowflake.
- Try making a paper fringe. Fold a long strip of paper in half lengthways. Make many cuts at right angles up to the fold line.
- When your child has made a collage to be proud of, you could spray it with gold or silver paint to make an attractive calendar.
- Do leaf rubbings by covering different shaped leaves and ferns with paper and rubbing across them with wax crayons. Cut out your wax leaves and stick them onto a large piece of paper arranged to look like a tree.

Creative development

Model making and craft activities

Using a variety of materials will help your child to learn more about shape and space. Modelling is a tactile and creative activity and will help to increase your child's imagination and confidence.

Collect together a range of materials:
- cardboard tubes from gift wrap;
- egg cartons, grocery packets and containers;
- unusually shaped boxes, for example circular or hexagonal;
- wool, cotton and fabric;
- paper, cardboard and picnic plates;
- glue, parcel tape and a stapler.

Modelling and craft projects
- Make a boat from the bottom of an egg carton (for the hull), a cardboard tube (funnel), string (ropes) and gummed paper shapes (portholes and flags).
- Design your own musical instrument – for example, a shaker can be made by filling a clean yoghurt pot with rice, pasta, dried peas or lentils. Place another pot on top and tape together securely. Or make a drum from an upturned pan or tin and use a wooden spoon as a beater.
- A spider can be made with an individual segment from an egg box, with pipecleaner legs.
- Measure round your child's head and staple a band of card to fit. Use a paper plate as a face and attach ears and whiskers to make an animal mask.
- Puppets are fun to make – a simple hand puppet bear can be made from a paper bag. Screw up the corners to make ears and draw on eyes, nose and mouth with felt pens. Or make a mouse from a cone of thick paper or thin card with two holes for your child's fingers to be the front paws. Stick on cardboard ears, pipecleaner whiskers and a wool tail.

- For a good introduction to sewing, and the idea of going in and out with a needle, just stitch with wool and a tapestry needle through a clean polystyrene food tray. When your child is confident with this, draw a simple outline picture for them to sew round. If necessary, help them by making holes 2cm apart. Later, you could ask them to stitch round the letters of their first name.
- You can buy commercially produced playdough for modelling, or make your own with two cups of plain flour, one cup of salt, one tablespoon of cooking oil and some food colouring. Just mix well and use! Keep airtight in plastic bags, with each colour separate.

Make-believe and role-play

Most children, when given a few toys, will soon become involved in make-believe. Your child will play imaginatively with a range of toys and household objects in a variety of settings (see the suggestions opposite for ideas). You can be involved by playing another character, or you could sit back and make suggestions or ask questions. It is important to accept your child's ideas and be sensitive to what they want to imagine – don't impose your own ideas!

Outside activities can stimulate role-play:
- The sandpit can become a building site with diggers and dumper trucks.
- Your child can be the captain of a ship with a boat or container in the paddling pool.
- Ride-on toys can make your child a racing driver, fire-fighter or horserider.

Dressing up
A dressing-up box is always useful to have. Collect a range of hats, garments, accessories and props. Vary what is put in the box from week to week. Cramming everything in can be confusing for young children, and too much to handle. Your child will learn about different people's traditions if you include a selection of items from other cultures wherever possible.

Playing house
You will need:
- a corner that can be screened off;
- small items of furniture or boxes;
- dolls and soft toys, and their clothes;
- dressing-up clothes for your child;
- a doll's pram or cot;
- imitation food and empty food packets;
- cups, saucers, plates, teapot, jug and cutlery;
- kitchen equipment and household items.

Shopping
Let your child decide which type of shop they want to make, and help them to collect together the necessary equipment.

All shops will need:
- purses and wallets;
- realistic toy money;
- a shopping bag or basket;
- price labels;
- a cash register or box for the money;
- a table for a counter and shelves for display.

Examples of things to sell at different shops:
- corner shop – empty packets and jars;
- greengrocer – real or pretend fruit and vegetables;
- jeweller – old costume jewellery, beads and brooches;
- florist – tissue paper or plastic flowers and plants.

For a more complicated game, you could set up a supermarket complete with a toy trolley.

Hospital play
This is always popular, and can also be useful if your child or a member of the family is due to be hospitalised. It can help to dispel some of the natural worries that your child may have about what might happen during an illness.

You will need:
- a child-sized bed and covers;
- bandages and plasters;
- a clipboard and toy phone;
- a toy stethoscope and thermometer;
- scales for weighing a baby doll;
- nurses' and doctors' dressing-up clothes, including a surgical mask.

Physical development

Physical play and activities enable children to develop their co-ordination and balance. They help to ensure children's health and wellbeing as well as being rich learning opportunities.

The following activities all promote the improvement of children's gross motor (whole-body movement) skills:
- walking;
- running;
- hopping;
- jumping;
- skipping;
- climbing;
- throwing and catching;
- stretching, bending and curling up tight;
- dancing;
- swimming;
- riding a bike or scooter.

Outdoor play

Children benefit from playing outside as often as possible, especially when the weather is fine. It gives them more freedom of movement and the fresh air is good for them! Your local park will have a range of activities available, but you can set up a variety of physical play opportunities in your own garden quite easily. Examples include:

Ride-on toys
Children find ride-on toys great fun and they are good for developing co-ordination. You could set out a 'road' round part of the garden, making it different each day, using household equipment such as a bucket or washing-up bowl for a roundabout.

Ball games
There are lots of games that you can play with your child and they are good for developing ball skills that improve co-ordination, including:
- kicking and passing a football;
- throwing and catching balls of different sizes;
- aiming at a junior basketball ring or empty bucket;
- hitting a ball with a cricket or baseball bat.

Obstacle courses
Make an obstacle course in the garden. Encourage your child to help by coming up with ideas for this. The obstacle course could include:
- a rope to jump across;
- a big box open at both ends to scramble through;
- an old tyre to jump into and out of.

If you have a climbing frame, slide or swing, these could be incorporated in the course. Make the course fairly easy to begin with, and then gradually increase the difficulty as your child's skills improve.

Rubber tyres
These can be used as a swing (hung from a tree), for climbing through, rolling or to sit in (as a pretend road vehicle, train or boat).

A sandpit

Commercially-produced sandpits are available, but an old sink or large plastic container three-quarters full of fine sand will do just as well. You could provide a few different sizes and shapes of container and spoons or spades to dig with.

Don't forget to cover the sandpit securely at night to prevent animals from soiling the sand.

A paddling pool

Your child can find out what floats and what sinks, as well as enjoying splashing about in the water themselves and sailing toy boats. Paddling pools are also good places for pouring and emptying water from a variety of containers.

ALWAYS be sure that your child is fully supervised when playing in or around the paddling pool, no matter how shallowly it is filled.

Indoor play

Some of the same ideas can be adapted for use indoors, depending on what space you have available. There are also gymnastics sessions available for very young children in many areas, or you could find out where your nearest soft-play facility or swimming baths are.

Construction play

This type of play is useful in developing children's fine motor skills (co-ordination of hand and eye movements) and their concentration span. Construction needs plenty of room. If the weather is fine, it is an ideal outdoor activity. However, a reasonable amount of floor space in your hallway, your child's bedroom or the living room will do equally as well. Often your child will want the construction left out for another day. A smaller table-top model could be worked on for many days!

Some good construction toys:
- Duplo®, Lego® or other interlocking bricks;
- plastic Meccano®;
- Stickle bricks;
- Quatro™;
- road and town layouts;
- large-scale train tracks;
- wooden blocks;
- cardboard boxes;
- planed planks of wood.

Your child could start by building the following:
- towers;
- houses;
- castles;
- forts;
- bridges;
- a lighthouse;
- a spaceship;
- a fire-engine.

It is a good idea to have some toy cars, figures and animals handy for imaginative play once the construction is completed.

Early Learning at Home | Schofield & Sims

Physical development

Physical development

Promoting body awareness

Body awareness is an important part of children's physical development, and contributes to their personal development too. Talk to your child about being healthy and growing up:
- eating healthy food;
- having enough sleep;
- taking exercise;
- keeping clean and avoiding germs;
- growing taller and stronger.

The following games and activities will promote your child's body awareness.

Creative and practical activities:

- Make a Growing-up Book – talk about what your child did from birth onwards. Use a double-page spread of a large scrapbook for each year of the child's life. Together, you and your child can stick in family photographs, pictures drawn, souvenirs from visits and early examples of the child's writing.

- Use a 'How tall am I?' chart to record your child's growth – attach a strip of paper to a wall or door in the kitchen or your child's bedroom. Date and mark your child's height in centimetres. Measure your child regularly every three to six months and mark the new height each time. Your chart could match the theme of the room or reflect a particular interest of your child. For example, if your child likes animals, the height chart could be in the shape of a giraffe.

- Design a Healthiness Chart – add columns such as 'Games I play', 'Healthy things I eat' and 'Hours I sleep' to a big sheet of paper. Put a photo of your child in the centre or at the top. Then stick on pictures cut from magazines or catalogues to illustrate healthy foods and activities. You could use clocks to show the times your child goes to bed at night and gets up each morning.

- Make a Body Puppet – first discuss different parts of the body and point to and name them. It is fun to do this in front of a mirror. You can then use an action figure or doll to show which parts of the body move, relating this back to your child's body. Use a large full-length photograph of your child if you have one (or of one of the child's favourite cartoon or television characters if not). Stick it onto card and cut round the picture. Cut the figure at the joints, then rejoin with split pins. Discuss and name the parts that move.

Songs, rhymes and action games:

- As you say or sing this rhyme, point to each part of the body as it is mentioned.

    Head, shoulders, knees and toes, knees and toes;
    Head, shoulders, knees and toes, knees and toes;
    Eyes and ears and mouth and nose;
    Head, shoulders, knees and toes, knees and toes.

- Jack-in-a-box jumps up!
    (Jump up and stretch to the sky.)
    Jack-in-a-box goes flop!
    (Flop down, but still standing.)
    Jack-in-a-box goes round and round!
    (Turn round.)
    And the lid goes down with a plop!
    (Drop to the ground, curled as if in the closed box.)

- One person says, "Simon says jump up and down." The other has to do the action. Continue, "Simon says…" followed each time by a different action. To make it harder, include some instances where you say, "Do this!" and demonstrate an action. The other should not carry out the action. If they do, they become the leader and the game starts again.

Published by Schofield and Sims Ltd,
Dogley Mill, Fenay Bridge,
Huddersfield HD8 0NQ, UK

Tel 01484 607080
www.schofieldandsims.co.uk

First published in 2006
Copyright © Schofield and Sims Ltd 2006

Author: Sally Johnson

Sally Johnson has asserted her moral right under the Copyright, Designs and Patents Act, 1988, to be identified as the author of this work.

British Library Cataloguing in Publication Data

A catalogue record for this book is available from the British Library.

All rights reserved. No part of this publication may be reproduced or transmitted in any form or by any means, electronic or mechanical, including photocopying, recording or duplication in any information storage and retrieval system, without permission in writing from the publisher.

Design by Ledgard Jepson
(www.ledgardjepson.com)

Printed in the UK by Wyndeham Gait Ltd.,
Grimsby, Lincolnshire

ISBN 0 7217 0908 7